Reception at the
Mongolian Embassy

Reception at the Mongolian Embassy

poetry and translations by

Nicholas Kolumban

A New Rivers Abroad Book

NEW RIVERS PRESS · 1987

Grateful acknowledgement is given to the editors of the following periodicals in which some of these poems first appeared:

Chariton Review, Cutbank, Hawaii Review, Michigan Quarterly Review, New Letters, Poetry Review, Blue Unicorn, Croton Review, Images, Lips, Greenfield Review, Northwestern Review, Porch, Poetry Now, Mozgo Vilag (Hungary), *Nyugati Magyarsag* (Hungary), *Szivarvany* (Chicago), and *Eletunk* (Hungary).

Reception at the Mongolian Embassy has been produced with the aid of grants from the First Bank System Foundation and the National Endowment for the Arts (with funds provided by the Congress of the United States).

New Rivers Press books are distributed by

The Talman Company	and	Bookslinger
150 - 5th Avenue		213 East 4th St.
New York, NY 10011		St. Paul, MN 55101

Reception at the Mongolian Embassy has been produced in the United States of America for New Rivers Press (C.W. Truesdale, editor/publisher) 1602 Selby Ave., St. Paul, MN 55104 in a first edition of 1,000 copies.

This book is dedicated to
Carolyn Forché, Louis Simpson,
and Daniel Simko

CONTENTS

III

I

Immigrants
Wrestling With
Sounds

JAROSLAV

This evening frightens me.
First, smoked sausage and bacon eaten with fingers
then dirty jokes,
your mouth with its gold-tooth blemish.
Later another man comes into the kitchen—
he has a goatee, roguish eyes,
is drunk, kisses your wife on the cheek.
He speaks in a foreign language.
Then you scream at him in English about "family shame,"
you whose family is a pick-up truck.
As he leaves
I make the connection between the goatee and your wife.
After several glasses of white wine
(with its calming, blond shimmer),
the three of us sit down on a sofa—
you, your wife and me, the instant counselor.
You two jabber about making love while the children howl,
about choking each other,
stuffed cabbage charred to coal on the stove.
Torn-out chair legs.
A swung leather belt. How it hurts.

My head turns from one to the other.
I shudder. Drink more wine.

ELEGY FOR THE UNEMPLOYED

I sit on my back porch at noon,
admire the neighbor's garage
bleached by sunlight.
The song of chilled crickets
and the whisper of birds in a pine.

I think of work
as others think of ice cream.
I want to stuff my mouth with it,
gorge myself on toil,
bathe in sweat;
but I just sit and think.
Time fills my hair,
gets under my fingernails
as ecstasy once did.

I want to be a connoisseur
of flag-red sweaters,
a dye-maker,
or fabricate cages
so we can import the shrieks
of pets indoors;
weld pipes, declare them leak proof
so heat can invade basements.
I want to build a wind machine
that takes deep breaths.

AT A PARTY

They want to petition the Hungarian government
to intercede for a Czech.
This Czech is really a Hunky, an engineer.
Petition and new schemes are born
in exiles who drink champagne in America.
I listen, praise Czechoslovakia,
the only democracy in Eastern Europe
after World War I. But *no* I'm told—
they had beaten Hungarians silly
in jails and boiler rooms
while sipping Asti Spumante.
A man turns fifty at the party.
His woman's hands slip under his shirt;
only his sideburns are gray
though he's pale in May
and his face sags.
I refill my plastic mug.
A woman broods about the soul's refusal
to leave the body.
I once saw a dead man in a movie:
they fitted him with plugs
for his ears, nose and anus,
a way to trap the soul!
I eat glorious Dobos torte,
a flour creation with subversive chocolate.
I admire a woman not my age.
She has a pug nose,
fine brown hair. A Renaissance coiffure.
Her breasts are modern, small,
knitted into the sweater.

AMSTERDAM

You two drink beer on a bench next to a *gracht*,
the water is thick and apple green
It exudes peace, not sadnesses
(your specialty)
People reside on boats on this immobile river
The roofs as flat as the water
the thin aluminum chimneys slick penises
You look for her who whipped you in your youth—
maybe she's the one on the cobblestone carpet of the square . . .

Why is she still the envoy of hope,
a marvellous figure of sex?
A recurring daydream: you stop
at the sight of an accident
a woman is dying   it's her
You clutch her to your chest
her wound drenches you
Your shirt weeps on top of her blouse, united
You mourn for both of you
But Amsterdam soothes—
your friend and you drink beer on a bench next to a *gracht*
He presents the oddities:
rubber tiles that cushion children's knees
as they fall from a swing,
hitching posts along the narrow sidewalks
to protect the pedestrians
It's magically good to roam with a childhood friend
who urges you to be merry,
wants you to have more real beer or women—
the ones in shopwindows,
ornaments,
under red light bulbs

You're in awe of the city, of the fairy tale houses
(two windows shape an entire floor)
the lace curtains with their pink souls,
the trusting cats—
creatures that cured your aversion
to non-humans

You accept what excites your thoughts,
takes your melancholy and bleaches it gently
in the water of the canals

IMMIGRANTS WRESTLING WITH SOUNDS

The blackboard is parcelled like a small farmer's field,
the chalk bleached like medicine.
It's hard to write clearly, hard to teach
in this small room where the pupils are old
and pressed against the wall.
They wield heavy tongues.
Some had resided for years in the House of English.
The moustached teacher speaks impeccably, with an accent.
You need an accent to know how to make one fade.
The goal is to scribble over their mother tongue.
The class yearns to say "thigh" but it comes out "sigh,"
their teacher sculpts a thigh in the air
but makes do with "Thai,"
a wild dish with curry and coconut.

A new arrival stares at the teacher,
she has dark hair under her yellow strands
and fragile shoulders.
Her eyes shine with blunt fever,
she can say "winter" like Farah Fawcett
and has the figure of a novice nun.

WHY WHAT WHEN WHERE flutter in the room
as VHY VHAT VHEN VHERE.
Old folks won't purse their lips
without their mates.

Who has a dog? Listen to one.
Learn to howl discreetly.
Don't buy an immigrant dog.

FRESH SNOW

For *Janos Olah*

Snow rolls off the roof.
Snowflakes play tug of war in the schizophrenic breeze.
The house opposite mine blazes princely yellow.
Its shape is a child's block—
I want to haul it under my arm.
I believe I'm not in America,
in this silent, whitewashed world
where there's freedom to speak up
but not to be heard.
No one is anointed by warmth.

I'm back in Austria, a child in the mountains
during World War II,
gazing out an open window,
touching flakes with my tongue.
I want to be snow, be white like snow,
dissolve my color in it like a cat,
like a flag that promises obedience.
I want to hug a snowdrift to chill my cheeks
that were burnt by math assignments.
I want to inhale the strong spirits
of snow
that stun you like rum.

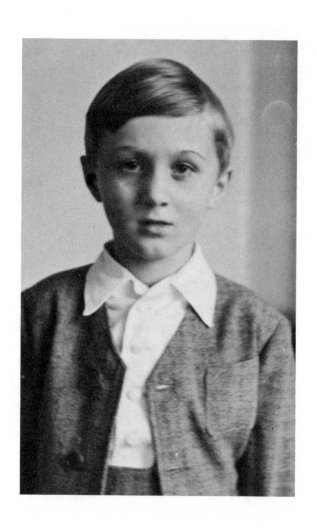

THE IMMIGRANT

America, you welcomed me,
my pock-marked fingerprints,
my unearthly short trousers

You gave me a professor who bellowed
when I wrote "lard" instead of "Lord"
A woman who revered my shirtless chest,
its fragrance,
but dismissed my love
You gave me arthritis that could be viewed in my eye,
a wounded neck that healed
Glorious London broil, queer broccoli

Schaefer beer, this doctor of insom
You give me a lump in my throat
when I see your lovely, alien flag
A bad town
where people vanish
inside their two-bedroom tombs
Only the birds are willing to speak

America, America
one day I'll leave you
(won't love your rude school children anymore,
won't mow your lawn)
for my backyard
where freedom rests
on prickly branches

TWO AGES

My daughter thinks that the boogeyman is old.
When I ask her for his age
she says six and four.

We all have two ages.
The first is the gift of birth
and the other carries the spirit of the moment.

Peter, sitting under a tree invaded by Japanese beetles,
curses their appetite.
The gray hairs on his chest stand on end.

He must be 50 and 70.

His wife cuts me black-eyed Susans from the garden.
She bends slowly toward the stems;
she wears a bikini. Her waist sports a Florida tan,
the crowfeet of her navel flash a smile.

She's 48 and 19.

AIDED BY THE LANGUAGE OF MORNING

The gruff, throaty complaints of blue jays,
the voice of an irate crow
transport me to my European birthplace.
The factual conversations of dogs, the harsh might
of trucks as speed shakes the engine,
the man-made thunder of jets as it cuts the flesh of the wind—
these reverberate in my memory.
They mesmerize me with the sounds of my childhood.
Budapest is the acoustical twin of Somerville:
the rhythmic exaltations of crickets; tires
sizzling in the rain;
buses speaking with the blunt throttle of low-flying planes—
both tongues untranslatable.
I live in Budapest though I reside in Somerville.
As I age, I live more in Budapest,
aided by the language of morning
and my mind which seeks to recover my history,
my splintered past.

A GUINEA AFTERNOON

I took my guinea pig for a spin in the park.
I let the flat-footed jester wade in grass,
munch on the taller blades.
He followed me to the picnic table.
With less relish, he grazed on the green paint.
A woman joined us, read a novel;
she held the pages as if flirting with them.
I showed her my pet.
The woman's deep-set eyes sparkled,
her thin face shone in the afternoon sun.
She had lovely, childlike hips,
kept her head tilted like a deer.
We constructed metaphors:
a miniature cow, a benign rat.
No, look at his nimble nose: a rabbit cow!

The woman lived alone, kept avocado plants for pets.
Loved to make soup.
I told her I craved bone soup with marrow
but she just shrugged, held hands with her novel.

I would have gladly visited her, praising her Afghan rug.
Cupped her curved breasts.
I would have grazed on her intoxicating moss.

AT A WEDDING

You drive up to the country club
where weddings flourish now,
elbow your way to the largest stuffed mushroom,
bite chunks off the salty, gray cheese
nobody wants.
You saunter through the building alone,
as if you were still a bachelor.

A woman in the food line is strange.
Her hair is wind-blown
here where there's no wind.
The rouge on her cheeks fingerprints.
Her eyes are blue and perpetually amazed.
Her large breasts sway
like church bells in the spring.

You stare at the turkey,
its thighs garnished with red roses.
The petals resemble a maze.
You steal a rose, transplant it
to your ashtray,
moistening it with beer.
You're unable to eat,
staring at the flower,
longing to conjure
an image out of it.
The bride and groom grope
for each other's mouths
(the tongue's journey in a maze),
reacting like marionettes
to the soprano of the crystal.

ABANDONING MY PROFESSION

All of you leave me.
One by one I cross out your names.
You turn in your books, kiss the battered bindings,
twirl records on your fingertips to hear the guttural voice.
I shut the top windows of my room with a pole,
eat melted chocolate from March
and lock my filing cabinet.
I erase pencil marks on the desks
but the "fuck yous" I preserve
in alcohol. I remove tacks from my pants,
pocket a piece of chalk, so I can write
on the grass, my green board.
I crawl through a hole in the wall
and mount a mule. She sings!
I turn in the saddle as I leave
and wave to the building's flat roof:
it's littered with bottles, torn blankets.
I count four rubbers, make love to my mule.
She keeps on singing about her father.
At ease, I watch the sunset,
the red eye diving into the bruised, dark lake
where I will stay.

A SCHOOL SUPERVISOR

You've become unspeakably thin
and the growth on your skull
has lost its luster.
A bald spot, an assault of the skin,
makes you look Japanese.
You're wilted, ashen.

I'm amazed that you mean your smile,
that it's not forced.
Anger left your eyes, time has cleared your pupils.
You don't have to call the principal now—
there's no shouting match.
I don't refuse your commandments.

My daughter is selling you a wreath,
meant for the door, not for a coffin.
You want her to return;
your good will makes me ashamed.
Are you lonely?

I might cross the bridge
my daughter builds with her effervescence.

Who knew that in teaching
there could be pain.

THE RESCUE

The smoke alarm wails like a pig
with a jackknife stitched in its throat.
I roll out of bed, weak from rum.
Who touched off this alarm?
Not bacon or London broil, it's much more serious.
My house is burning!
I'm not Cocteau, I'm not saving the flame.
I kick out the screen like a bear,
shake the woman beside me, run to get Nicole
with her bruised toe, dolls and scream.
I get my manuscript that I raised in a metal box
without water because it thrives on patience and soot.
I rescue my long-necked shoehorn, good for stirring drinks.
I rescue my self in my own arms
so I can listen to the tremulous crickets
that are always with me.
The people are not there.

MY LIFE ROLLS BEFORE ME IN A DATSUN

On the way home from New Plague, Arizona
my odometer peeled off years, memories

1956 — I left my country, my first love
          She hurt her spine in a fight
          but I didn't stay   I couldn't heal her
          I abandoned her for a plane—
          snowfield-clouds, gray dunes of ocean

1961— I exchanged my mother tongue for American food,
          downed milk, dissected novels,
          mowed my long hair, fixed my mouth in a grin
          I forged muscles in a small room from weights
          Took numerous showers to be worthy of this land

1973— My son's head appeared
          His sweet temple was bloody
          My gratitude spilled over: I married
          I cooked—I dyed our house salmon
          the most bewitching color

1989— I recorded echo fugues,
          collected woodpecker holes
          Guzzled thimblesfull of Saint James rum—
          it's square, crystal-heavy bottle,
          etched with the braille of the drunk

2011— My chosen year of demise
          I stepped off a non-military jet
          still in motion over the Atlantic
          without my first defense, Father's parachute,
          which I always carry

ELLIS ISLAND

Drains in the middle of the stone floor.
The rooms are paved with tiles—
in another life they were bathrooms.
Immigrants slept here:
the walls were hosed down when they left,
the chemicals seething like their memories.

In the Great Hall doctors scanned the arrivals,
sitting in judgment over lameness, trachoma,
tuberculosis.
A six-year old was marked
with an E for a bad eye;
her mother hid the spot
to save the child from deportation.

Clerks played parents:
they baptized an Austrian Jew Sean Ferguson
because he said *schon vergessen,**
a Hungarian farmer was named Doug Kennedy
when he mumbled *de kell enni.**
A Chinese became Sam Tin;
he loved to eat canned sardines.

Up on the roof
the cupolas loom like helmets of German gendarmes;
milk weed and poison ivy bloom on the field
where the immigrants had played ball.
They couldn't grasp how to swing,
how to run in a circle.
Their strange gloves slipped off,
the feet yearned to kick leather.

The Statue of Liberty suns herself,
wearing her loose, green summer dress,
her muscular arm uncovered.
Her back turned to Ellis Island.

* *schon vergessen* means *I've forgotten* in German
de kell enni means *I'm hungry* in Hungarian

II

A Globe-Trotting Shudder

MIDNIGHT

Sándor Csoóri

The tender elderberries grow in the dark.
I'm walking toward the cemetery.
I'm half-drunk and look shabby, lost,
like the old poets.

This is how the moon roams with a diamond violin
in a bad novel.
A bat travels low.
I only hear the moans of a sick thrush
at the bottom of a hedge.
He's delirious.

I mourn you, then lay mourning aside.
I begin to sing. Watch the clouds
sprint by at a breakneck speed.
I must think of you, constantly,
you, who now can't be imagined.
Like the world's afternoon,
like the wound of air around my mouth.
Words whisper to me in the dark: you were fiery.
Others say: you were the memory of a dirt road
where I groped blindly.
The lewd imprints of your feet
are still visible in the dust
that can't be resurrected.

But these are words—
the heartbeat of *nothing* in me,
words that go to their death
like I go to mine
when I'm next to you
at night
on the road of elderberries.
In the heavy dust.

YOU MAKE A POOR SKY DWELLER

Sándor Csoóri

I can only see your body,
your mountain of hair
in the wind and in the hospital bed.
I only know the things you love,
the things you let get close to you
during these quickly passing days.

Broken glass on the hillside reflects you
above the mud.
You stroll in the scaled down sky, look around intently;
you're more clumsy in this bird and cloud traffic
than on Ferenc Boulevard.
You make a poor sky dweller and I've known this.

Wild grass, wild hollyhocks, weeds from Matra mountain
suit you nicely.
Streaming rocks, streaming water.
Lewd basil, a bell's clamor rolling around
on the floor of the forest,
not the kind that lays you into wind's coffin.
You could even seduce ladybugs, an oakleaf!

There's no other womanly body for me, no other womanly smile.
You remained a nomad like the wind
like a blackthorn bush on its wedding night.
Tomorrow you'll step on grass barefooted and I'll become soft.
What do I care if the world is reduced to splinters
or is solid like brass?
There might be a war—
future's ruins are wobbling.
The sky wears dark glasses — generals in a coup.
Even if I have to sleep with bullets, you'll be close to me.
My fingers keep vigil on your throbbing vein.

AS IF I WERE WAITING FOR SOMEONE

Sándor Csoóri

The moon shines into my room.
It scrubs the wooden floor, so it glitters.
One can see the graveness of the splinters.
I pace from the window to the door;
I have been doing it for hours;
as if I were waiting for someone at a railroad station
in the provinces. I'm not certain
am I waiting for you after your miserable defeat,
waiting with Dostoevski's heart on loan
when silence and agoraphobia hold me in their tenacious grasp.

Maybe you don't quite exist,
only your body still pulsates after the verdict,
your body that outlives everything.
Your many hairpins and barrettes glitter at me.
What did you lust for, you joyless predator—
money, fame, unearthly debauchery?
Did you lust for a highway, hemmed with burning trees,
that leads to heaven?
Only the chilled light remains from the triumphant flames,
only an uncertain shiver inside the body
as if I were waiting perpetually for someone.

THE IMPRINT OF FERNS,
CRISSCROSSED WITH BRANCHES AND TWIGS

Sándor Csoóri

Spring has arrived. It's returned again.
I break off the rotting branches of walnut trees.
They crack one after the other like pistol shots.

Spring has arrived. It came with the Easter bees,
April's lechers. The golden gate is flung open,
clear to its hinges. Anybody who cares to, can slip through it.

The old poets send messages—
you should learn a new language, more billowy sighs.
Everything is an open window: the mouth of a joyous poem!

The crematorium's smoke is a long sentence, reaching up to the sky.
Penitently, it lifts from inside us, remaining slender.
We implore our loveliest dead: forgive us that we're still breathing!

Spring has arrived. War-mongering news dances behind it,
slapping its heels, flashing its spurs
like a skeleton on stilts at the Carnival of Rio.

There's blood on the floor of the blood-orange forests,
blood under the eyes of planes, in the Saharan dust.
Blood around the resilient beds of mothers who bear armies.

Spring has arrived again. From among the revived butterflies,
rolled-up newspapers (with skulls and crossbones) bear down
on us, too, but we've forgotten to be afraid.

Come what may, this season is already happening to me:
the earth preserves in me the imprint of a blooming forest
as amber does the ferns with crisscrossed branches and twigs.

HERMIT SUMMER

Sándor Csoóri

The roofless summer nights are peaceful.
You don't hear whining grindstones from over the barn.
Or crying from above.
You don't hear the screeching of public speakers
awakened from their sleep in the shrill light.

It's like the night after creation.
Dew strolls around the umbrella-like flowers
of wild carrots,
then falls by itself like a glass from a bar
in a silent movie.

The leaves of thick cherry trees barely quiver.
Is music being born? A breeze?
Have a fruit picker's hands been left behind
in the branches?
You saw many, many abandoned hands during the war.

You go from hedge to hedge, from blade to blade.
Every heartbeat is an assent:
You only want this renewable silence of a summer evening.
The night-breathing of insects in the tired grass.

Grasshoppers, leaping fish could have invented God
during such an evening.
Water and stars are too far apart—
they had to think of something to bring them closer.

The sky is open, the earth is open
to the four winds.
Beetles loiter in the roofless garden
hunting for lice on themselves.

They make you shiver but even this late shiver feels good.
You think of rocks in the sun.
Of warm wind.

HEAD BOWED

Sándor Csoóri

Autumn is coming.
You wait for it to happen with head bowed,
on a hill covered with sour cherry trees.
Maneuvers start today,
sweeping you into their middle—
this somber Mardi Gras of weapons and tank treads.

You want to stay relaxed throughout the year,
to burn weeds in the afternoon yard
as summer's worldly citizen
and drive this last butterfly herd under the parched hedges.
But you patter in the shriveled grass.
Waiting is empty like a cracked swallow's nest.

Autumn belongs to the armies,
their tanks destroying the immense blue—
filtered through a cobweb of ox spittle.
They're burglars, shattering a glass door with an axe.

Do you hear? Are Europe's bolted horses
stampeding toward you
with their wide, tense nostrils
as if the fists of warring death
would strike you again?

Someone whispers to you from behind a tree.
You always loved things that were lethal
and felt joy at protection, itself a threat.

Well, don't be joyful and don't love them.
At your ankles wild saffron and chicory
stretch eagerly toward the heights
as if sending messages to a planet eons away.

IN THE ROOT CELLAR

Sándor Csoóri

This is where you've ended.
You speak eloquently, although age-spotted, bent leaves
rustle in front of your words
and drop, with you, into the nothingness of autumn.

He who once listened to you shies away,
feeds long-haired dogs behind the door
like someone who thinks of his country
and a revolution as a failed nightmare.

Glances plummet under the wheels into the mud.
Here nobody wants to see anything,
not miracles, not blood, not even himself.
The faces of the famous beam

from newspaper debris under the bushes.
And the women, the lovely women who were fond of you,
are now feeble, dull. Their souls
are barren. They scan beyond the shaggy mountain

you face. You could turn into a baleful horse skull
in their eyes. Admit it, you're to blame
because you stayed freer than anyone else.
Gallingly free. You used to step over graves,

over crossing gates. Dig yourself into a root cellar now,
for the winter, into chilled silence
or into the elegy of a straw bed. The ice-solid soul
will thaw out, awakened by the loud spring waters.

A SECRET ASSIGNMENT

Sándor Csoóri

People are coming to scan my face.
They check the clouding of my sunken eyes.
Is there life in me
after a filthy hand assaulted me
with a knife? Is there a grin left
after the injury to my soul?

Cigarette smoke coils along the wall
up to the ceiling—
fraternal signal fires
warning villages
about the Turks
who came to loot, to murder.

Poplars hum in the wind
and a tired jet inches homeward.
They draw my eyes with them
but spaces open up unexpectedly in me—
border fortress autumn
battles for me on pastures, marked by ox trails.

I hear the crackling of straw,
the crackling of bones; bonfires
flutter from among the reed cones.
Pheasants escape (leaving their weed homes),
cherry-red blood gushing
out of beheaded corpses.

I lie in the pasture with my unhealed wound.
Clouds hover over me, alien soldiers on horseback come close.
Which of my many selves
do they trample into my native soil?
Mud, dung, snakeweed fill my mouth.
I retch from the sweet clumps of my country.

But I know the wind will reach me,
it will delicately pull my hair,
stroke the hands of the dead.
This touching makes me face all possibilities
like a secret assignment compels
the reluctant martyr.

THE FIRST TIME

Elemér Horváth

It was glorious to stay inside you,
you severe, green-eyed brunette
It was sublime that you brought me back to earth
that you spilled my blood
It didn't occur to me until now that there's death
The taste of immortality is salty
Kisses, July heat, blood, sweat flowing into my mouth
Thank you for pulling me back to earth
but paradoxically we ascended
This happened in a borrowed bed
in a shabby apartment
in a provincial capital
Thank you for not concealing your wrinkles
your warts and political convictions
We practically agree on things and I'm not young
What joy it is to love you through my senses!
To love you with your trimmed fingernails,
with your manicured short hair
You stand before me naked to your waist
wearing a hand-made skirt
You're a poetic patchwork
you formerly blond virgin
I'm pleased that you're so harsh in your desires
in your egoism so naively soothing
I don't know how long I live
but I know that now you're the most beautiful
in this godly light
inside this purgatory
You smile you bleed

50

EXECUTION

Elemér Horváth

Look, I take every revolution to heart
since the time I lost mine
I was young
maybe this is how I preserve youth
my audacious hope
that things will be altered
but now it's too late
your single gray hair is more momentous to me
than the martyrs of all movements
yesterday on June 19, 1983
the Iranian revolutionaries
executed three young girls
they were precisely the same age
as you when you first kissed me

IT'S TANGLED BUT ACCURATE

Elemér Horváth

Titmice eat on the snow-covered terrace
The cactuses flower in my dining room
I thrive according to a different timetable
between Grieg and Bartok
An earthquake rumbled on the radio last night
The Persian Foreign Minister landed in America
pondering the issues of oil refineries
The pope knocked on a nursery door
I've noticed I live on the periphery of public life
I only mingle if a snowstorm forces me to wield a shovel
It must have been ages since I made love
to the one I cherish
In the evening I read Durkheim
Suicide as a public act
Winter will be lengthy
according to several appraisals
The birds feel grandly at home on my terrace
I write poems with urgency and speed
like Wen Ting yun
at the end of the Dynasty

THE CLOAK OF PROTEUS

Elemér Horváth

extra hungariam
only nothing exists   the pulsing of cosmic waves
which can be the corn on the foot of the Tower of Pisa
   the uncreased forehead of the unicorn
   or the musical notes of the wise hummingbird
   the translucent rabbits of a glass hat

undoubtedly God throws dice
he plays freely   *ex machina*
he's identical with himself like the chameleon
as the coral that tingles on the spine of a fish
the star-filled sky on the owl's glasses

there's a crescent on my thumbnail   *mare serenitatis*
a small Buddha smiles on its surface
   only the Garden of Eden is rooted in the soil
   he who finds his homeland
   meets a "no trespassing" sign

My sail is the shreds of a discredited straight jacket
and while the wind (which saw the spirits)
blows behind me
   I'm the liquid fireworks
   the cross-legged position racing for its life
   the vagabond Spanish flue
   the monkey wrench with a puma's foot
into which I'm moulding myself
homo hungaricus

A CHEST WITH PAINTED TULIPS

Elemér Horváth

The soldiers burn down the village and they say
"this is victory." Those who try to argue with them
are immediately shoved against the wall. Everybody
quiets down because they see there's no wall.
The child would love to bang the door shut
but there's no door. Instead, he turns around,
using his heels. This gesture changes his life.

Thirty years later he returns from New York
to take a picture of the ruins. He notices awe-
struck that all the houses have doors. On the threshold,
the doors turn on their heels; they may not want to
argue with him. The family is in the middle
of the room, painting tulips on a chest. A soldier
stands at the wall and fixes them with his gun.
The child would love to put a match to all this
but he's already old. He lacks the strength.

A CONFESSION OF LOVE TO BUDAPEST

Sándor Csoóri

How much trash is whirled by the wind on the streets.
How many drained, vagrant faces;
a smothering streak of smoke under the city's sky.
How many eroded love affairs behind the walls!
If passion shifts into green like a stoplight,
the suppressed leaves and branches, the rain come alive.
It snows lace curtains.
A kind of bright lunacy darts along the tram rails;
it hoots, weeps like the falsetto of a flute.

Do I love you? Can I stand you?
I tear off the calendar's pages. Budapest, thirty years.
I wander your streets like a hobo. I have no direction.
Here everything is intimately closer to my hands, to my body,
closer to ecstasy, to murder.
Flames spew up in my face from the dragon mouth of boilers
as in a fairy tale. The timeless muck
in the sewers constantly streams.
Budapest, am I yours? Or only your prisoner?

Often I desert you, disown you but also pine after you.
You're where the fires lay down like exhausted cattle under yoke.
In your yard a porcupine saunters, an intimate of prehistoric earth.
Budapest, a million windows, your wrought iron, creak
in the velvet stirrings of the porcupine.
Your lovely neurotic women scream all alone.
I join them in mirrored elevators,
in the hair-floating draft of underground trains.
I'm multiplied by your innumerable glances
and my lunacy. If you don't let me in,

only a forest will ruminate along with me,
with death who's leaning on the moon.
Then the world will not help me in my need,
won't send news, won't wait for me, won't send me music
in which I can study immortality.
Budapest, you tremble alluringly on my membranes.
You tremble like peas on a drum to signal a threat
                                    from under the ground.
Will smoke kill me? An earthquake?
The rampant spreading of the rose petals of fire?
Even if I betray you, I'll be with you.

A GLOBE-TROTTING SHUDDER

Sándor Csoóri

This summer night is bright.
The nocturnal waters are bright.
One can clearly see a distant shiver pulling into the harbor
as if people's teeth were chattering
on the other side of the earth.

Helsinki sleeps flat on its back, stupefied with fatigue,
as someone who was struck by violent heat.
Only the feeble drunks cock their ears.
They sense this shiver, wanting to stuff
warm seagulls under their shirts.

Who knows what tomorrow has in store?
Maybe a new day with blooming roses that sprout up.
Ship debris lurks at the water's edge—
or is the blatantly proud collapse coming
like a barbaric heart attack but without prophets, public speakers.

Everything is close, even what was remote
as if there had been no distance, no time
as if we had not been waiting,
sometimes for centuries for one word
to claim the incognito future as ours.

Even a deep sigh was enough, the name of a new God.
Dreams of an ocean because life wanted to go on
and not only in grime, in the moment's stifling ecstasy.
Is it enough to live?
No, one must outlive even life!

Once the Finns strolled as guests at the mercy of the arctic light.
The trees grow goose pimples now from the cold.
The rocks freeze. Even the statues,
facing the ocean, feel a kind of globe-trotting shudder.
I bend down and stroke the water
like someone who can't help but love.

GLOWING EMBERS ILLUMINATE THE SNOW

Sándor Csoóri

I'm mired again in the horseshoe-shaped valley.
I haven't seen a human for days: I'm surrounded
by a fortress of snow.
Crows prowl around my hut,
at night a hallucinating fox.

Winter gives me what I always craved:
I can be alone and dazzled by the forest, by the mountain.
I gaze at the bony frame of nothing.
I can see the reflection of my cracked fingernails
in the tin-colored sky.

Huge, bleached bones float down the Danube.
I watch them as I would a movie.

The old ones who lived beyond the reach of memory,
my forefathers, unexpectedly stab me with pain
under the walnut tree, bent by snow.
Is a wolf chasing a flock of wild swans toward you?
The wind hurls snow.

It piles snow into the well, on the sill,
on the country roads, on the trashcans.
Clad in a ghostly sheet, the storm chops wood.
Its quick axe clinks; white shavings lift
toward the sky.

The chimney hums, the haystacks hiss.
A horse neighs gruffly in the barn,
Its grating sound wrenches you.
You realize that no paper, no God can reach you
through the snow until spring.

But I will get through! Even across time.
I'll be there in the steam of sweaty footrags
under the light-blue beams.
I'll peel back the husk of poverty with you.
I'll shell golden ears of corn.

Will I be your guest, your son? Or only a fugitive of the future?
A liberated nightmare that pleads for wine from your cellar,
drinks your world from your lips?
Your baked apple is tastier than Eden's!
Savoring it, one can hibernate until death.

Snowclouds discharge a ton of celestial thread.
I'll come by at night.
A log's glowing embers illuminate the snow.

THE SMELL OF CHILLED DUST IN MY NOSTRILS

Sándor Csoóri

The breeze, whipped up by cars, slaps me
on the January street. The smell of chilled dust
in my nostrils. It's like the smell of virile pepper,
pulverized in a mortar.
My head, heavy from it, ambles above the city.

This season is no fall, no winter, no spring.
It's rather the taut time of the castrati.
This is how measured ecstasy
drops to earth like vagrant bricks
in front of our eyes.

Now I should closet myself into my solitary, blind room
among my obdurate poems, among the past masterpieces
of massive snowfalls.
Only what I love should become reality!
God, lend me your lovely cloakrooms, filled with blizzards.

Lend me the eyes of foxes and hunters,
the eyes of wild geese, their unswerving glances as they drift
in the air. Lend me all the eyes that help the imagination
outlive our sly decay,
that help us survive this filthy earth time.

I feel the dust of January prickle my skin, my mouth
as if the dust of space had penetrated me, the dust
of some Saharan power. The kidneys, the liver hurt
with a dull ache but the mind, left to its own devices,
rambles inside grand snowfalls, euphorically.

III

The Native Tourist

THE TOURIST

He strolls down *Vaci* street
the shine of shopwindows doesn't reflect off his shoes
he sees the same books in all bookstores
sits under a Pepsi umbrella at the *Zserbo*
   his hazelnut ice cream melts like brown snow
later he listens to his belly groaning
   diarrhea—the legacy of Budapest
   he doesn't know what to eat
   even boiled fish causes him pain
   he doesn't know a doctor's address
he stares at women—their breasts wear exquisite buttons
there's no key to his room
   he must lean his suitcase against the door while he sleeps
his T shirt is drenched with sweat but he still wears it
   next day—armor against the sun
his bad eye is filled with the angry fumes of buses
in bed he writes postcards
   like someone who lights a cigarette again and again
his memory is singed
he stares at an old calendar on the wall
   that sports a Communist Donald Duck

LEAVING BUDAPEST

For *Miklos Beladi*

The dove above the Danube
soars like a slender, taut bridge
in the sunshine
I see the glowing cupola of the castle,
green like an abandoned copper breast

A girl with pointed heels
(a dove's beak)
dresses a shopwindow
Her pigtail pricks my eyes

A beggar sits in front of a store
her quivering hand points to her lap
strewn with coin fruit
enough for the winter
She took off her shoes in the July heat
Her feet are stiffened in an arc

I go to an outdoor cafe
watch a few workers disassemble the sidewalk
creating a hole
in which they disappear

The man who leaves at noon
drinks spritzer
and the bubbles speak
to him about the Danube
and the dove
and his desire to stay
a thousand years—
the length of his country's history

RESUME

Nicholas Kolumban was born and raised in Hungary.
When the war overran the peaks
of Transylvania, his parents fled
with fourteen suitcases, leaving such valuables
as two marzipan-loving goats
and Judith the horse.

He continued to grow in Reute, Austria
a village near the German front lines.
While the grownups were busy with building shelters
and making honey substitute
he attended Austrian schools,
learning about snow,
dialects and marmelade.
The daughter of the village clockmaker,
still in her teens, wished to make love to him,
but he declined, citing his youth.
Quite fluent in Tyrolian,
he and his parents—led by his father—
returned to Hungary. There he spent ten years,
finishing the math-burdened high school
and falling in love twice,
both times near water.

When bullets started again,
he hid behind a bathtub.
Soon, he rode a train to Austria.
Under the influence
of letters, he flew to America
by Tiger Airlines. This venture
took him 32 hours and stops.

He stayed for a while at Camp Kilmer,
getting fat on scrambled eggs,
jam and true honey.

He now teaches. He also loves
to bathe his dog in sockless feet
and let his toes be mistaken
for toy mice.

KNOWING YOU

You'd step with spikes
where my love lies bare

OCTOBER LIGHTS A MATCH

The car speeds like your thoughts.
The silos exude the aroma of childhood.
You stop before reaching her and turn back
as if she were a terrible hazard,
a lofty fence
and you the riderless horse.
The years haven't ripened her thighs
in you—
in your sleep you still stroke her fragile
shoulders, adore her jeweled posture.
The tips of her breasts,
proud pears,
curve upward.

October lights a match,
the edges of trees burn slowly, grandly.
Your being doesn't ignite,
it smolders yellow and fleshless.

MORNING REPORT FROM YOUR ROOM IN BUDAPEST

The warning flutes of owls wake you.
A few scattered coins on the floor,
telling the fortune you don't wish to know.
A thick, perfect cross faces you,
courtesy of your window.
You haven't even visited your parents'
graves which are holes in the wall.
Your parents are shrunk to ashes
as well as your will to see them.
You drove yesterday in an alien car,
the flashing lights of the dashboard
brought out the child in you:
you experimented with the brakes,
the seat belt.
You were rejected wherever you went; they demanded
to know what kind of celebrity you were.
Only professors had rooms at the conference.
You kept your importance hidden,
a bad habit of yours.
Anger flooded your eyes, you made a fist—
all men on earth deserve to sleep.
Poets have a lofty concept of justice.
But then you recalled why you came to this country:
to see your childhood
reflected in the mirror of houses,
in the terraces with their breathing geraniums.
The terrace on the fifth floor
where you faced a siren's rage
when bombs drilled holes in roofs.
You didn't mingle after the lecture in the crowd
that sipped sweet champagne,
chilled herbal juice.
You left with a thirst.

RECEPTION AT THE MONGOLIAN EMBASSY

from Budapest

I read the paper on a bench near the Danube
RECEPTION AT THE MONGOLIAN EMBASSY
THE YIELD OF THE WHEAT HARVEST
It doesn't say: EVA FALUDY DIED
killing herself in a picture-infested room.
She took the phone off the hook, silenced the doorbell,
gave her key to the super for his Monday discovery.
She wrote a note to her salt-white cat:
"I'm doing this because I'm blind."
But she could see the pills, her chalk jewelry.
She used a scarf to fasten her jaw to her upper teeth,
vain even in death.
Had 6000 forints in the bank—
a bus driver's monthly pay.
Her pension would be dinner for two at the *Intercontinental.*
There's a three-piece wardrobe in her room—
when she opened it, the door became wings,
a way to fly to heaven.

A trunk lay on top of her closet;
it was shrouded in bleached paper.
Even the color mourns her.

Godmother, you once made me a torte,
painting my mouth circus-white.
Sharpened my skates with a kitchen knife,
read about goats while Mother was away.
Now near the Danube, I see you with marbles under your lids.

Willful woman, arranging the smallest detail of your dying.
You left me behind.

HUNGARY

You're home.
They let in the exile
who loves the din of buses,
accepts the dark fuzz on women's legs.

You revere the harsh light of morning,
the thump of the first tram on the rails.
It's easy to forget the meanness of a cabby—
how heavy your suitcase was.
The box that tripped you in a store,
drawing blood.

In a bar you defend someone's right to sing
but a drunk gives you a shove:
"You're no Hungarian."
You down your draft wine
and feel sorry for yourself.
How can an accent rob you
of your nationality?

*

A debate at the Young Translator's Club.
People drink bitter beer
and sport the U.S. flag on their denims.
You plead for more buses and less bombs,
try to make a point in your mother tongue
but the words fail.
Your thoughts are conceived in English.

You scan a woman's face, silent and fatigued.
You mistake her sorrow
for a flicker of happiness.

76

OLD TIBOR OF HUNGARY

Lurk outside like a troll,
cut the grass, watch my window.
Yes, I'm home, deliver your gifts:
cornflowers, flushed apricots,
sweet, burning wine from the volcanic soil.
A bribe to listen to your life.

Soldiers destroyed your armor against poverty—
scissors, hairdryers.
You lived on unripe cherries, worked in a stone quarry,
flinging your sledgehammer with ease.
How frail you look now, lean and sinewy!
Sculpted veins on your arms, across your chest.
You warned your co-workers not to sing,
so they don't inhale the dust.
You buried them long ago.
Even you wheeze now, cough up soft pellets.

Your family is the shovel, the pickax,
your cousin the golden oriole
who invites his mate for a sour cherry snack.

For the hour you and I are father-and-son,
bonded by the resonance of your life in me
and by the amber bottle of wine
that shimmers lovingly in the sun.

IN THE DIMINISHING LIGHT

I curb my migraine with unearthly strong tea.
The pain crawls away from under my eye:
it brushes against the bone like a quill.
Objects begin to bloom around me: the loveliest flag.
It flaps grandly like my sleeves.
George's triangular hat on a pole
is smug about its shape.
George, a master craftsman of survival, doesn't realize
how lordly he looks, sitting erect in his yard.
He inhabits a thin nylon garment
that has the texture of a stocking, a mask that blurs.
He has been burnt.
His scarlet, knotted flesh is subdued in the dusk.
He's breathing pain, more momentous than my feeble one.
George believes I resemble an ancient poet with my mane,
thin sandals made of cordovan leather.
I look good on my invisible donkey—
my former self: lean and resolute.
To me he's a retired Prince Valiant, his wavy, gray hair
de-blonded, matted, having faced a succession of high noons.
He clutches an imagined, curved sword,
strangely benign.
His medicinal stocking has a line in the back like Romeo's
father's.
Velvet slippers guard his wounded heels.

A MAN

A man with a full mustache and white hair
leans back on a weak arm in bed.
His eyes are shut, the nose swollen
and strange as if pasted on.
For a moment he's a dozing walrus;
the giant pillow is a block of ice
covered with a foot of resilient snow.
He suns himself in the sick light
of the late afternoon.
A half-eaten roll remains on his plate.
His glasses are so strong, they read
the veins of wood in the table
where plastic bottles are scattered,
some overturned.
The man's cheeks are puffy.
Maybe he stores air in them
for the times his breath fails him.
The slits of his eyes mimic a smile.
The other arm is propped on the blanket
defiantly: the elbow is up in the air,
crooked but firm.
Where is this pose leading to?
Which arm will win out this afternoon,
this winter, in the light
that gleams on the iron bed?

POPPIES

I have a field of soft, unruly poppies.
Their petals are delicate, oily —
orange feathers
fluttering to the ground.

I've noticed, too, the indisputable signs
of diminishing life.
My glittering, burning poppies
thrive for two weeks
(a May life)
then turn gray at the edges, singed by decay.
Their stems are the fingers of the old.

I love to smell poppies
because they have no scent.
Their beauty is for my palm.
And for my eyes because I can still see.
Yes, our life is slipping away:
we should permit ourselves
to do almost anything.

SANDOR VADAY, WITH HODGKIN'S DISEASE

This wreath of herbs
on the bottom of my teacup mourns you.
You sprawl on your bed, dressed in a jacket
made of sackcloth.
Your woman has left you; I curl on the bed
cast for her 6'4" frame.
What a poor substitute I am,
babbling about the calm leaves outside.
I make tea, boil potatoes
and wolf down the drumsticks.
You eat like a tense sparrow.

You speak plaintively of your job
where you must browbeat men.
I listen and almost doze off,
something you can't do.

I see you, dear beanstalk,
toes gnarled, hair plucked by medication.

The glands swell along your breastbone,
pushing your lungs rudely aside,
making room for death.

THE VISIT

If you're hungry, I'd bring you
clean paper for a plate.
And more, if there's some.
But please leave something for me,
I'm always hungry.

Attila Jozsef

There's a knock. Attila Jozsef walks in
with his thin neck and wild Adam's apple.
I ask him to take a seat and to talk
about Paris. He sits in my favorite rocker,
the one with the delicate bars.
He sways to and fro, telling me
the concierge didn't allow cooking in the rooms.
He bit into croutons on windowsills
on the way to the Louvre.
(The pigeons gave him a dirty look.)
Wild geese seemed nervous in the park
as they held soggy pieces of bread.
I offer him tomato cabbage.
He shakes his head: "Since June I've only eaten wood."
He points at the rocker with his bony knee.
I nod, have too much respect for his poems.
He begins to eat while unscrewing the bars
meticulously. His sparse mustache quivers
with each bit. The sunken cheeks fill.
He chews the wood as I chew bacon,
spits out the gnarled pieces
and comments on the poor quality of varnish.
The armrests give him some trouble.

When he's finished, I hand him
a napkin and help to remove
two splinters from his gums.
He thanks me and promises a poem
on my mother's birthday.
He kisses me on the temple and leaves.

BUDAPEST

I'm above the Danube in a rented room.
Pictures of menacing birds.
I hear an owl or a seagull,
drink thick red wine,
this patron of weak stomachs.
Eat gingerly lean ham
not to violate my intestines.
I'm an alien who speaks the language
but stumbles on the rocks of custom.
Only a few talk to me—
I could as well be in London.
I give myself pep talks, praise my walrus
mustache. My loud shirt
that never wrinkles
unlike my moods.
I watch soap-white women dash toward the Metro.
Hard-assed, in high heels.
With every step
their legs quiver like aspic.

I lock my room while I take a shower,
then admire the view—
a glittering necklace hovers on the Danube.
A taut, lit-up bridge.

In the next room two whores whisper
in German, unaware
that I can understand.
The last customer has left, a noisy Japanese.
Now *they* kiss—
the popping of champagne bottles.

I'm above the Danube in a rented room.

A NATIVE TOURIST IN HUNGARY

My daughter is asleep with her chin propped in her palm.
She's a relative of Kant, an inventor of thoughts.
Is she contemplating the absence of playmates,
the food that makes her cough?
Her father's gibberish that he has never forgotten.
The incomprehensible shop talk of restaurants.

*   *

My friend escorts me to his kitchen,
this lair of intimacies where friendships are nurtured
and revived.
Sour cherries bloom in the artificial light
above the table. The pits are the color of human gums.
I empty the bowl while we ruminate about sailing—
an activity that is alien to me (I was born clumsy).
We praise skating, heating gasoline, burning sulfur
stuck in apartment locks—
things we had indulged in as childish rascals.
My friend has a scar from the bridge of his nose to his chin.
He received it while dueling cancer, aided by the doctor's blade.
His tan mutes the horror.

I've just arrived from America
and behave like a native tourist—
I walk the cobblestone rugs of Budapest, filming
the indolent Danube
that today has only eyes for basking in the sun,
not to work, to scrub the cement feet of bridges.
I relive my childhood—
I stand on the still vacant lot where I battled players
with my feet. I robbed them of the ball.
I touch the building where Father struggled in the sweatshop
of life.
I go and sit on the stairs below the docks like a lulled teenager
and listen to the European river.
It splashes gently in many tongues
to appease the bickering nations that live along its banks.
I spit inside the shining rails, the two banks that convey the Danube
let a part of me travel the width of my original country,
to stay here, to dissolve there
in my clandestine homeland.

BIOGRAPHICAL NOTES

Nicholas Kolumban, a native of Hungary, is a naturalized U.S. citizen. He received an M.A. from Pennsylvania State University and teaches English and creative writing to adults and children. His poems and translations have appeared in about eighty literary magazines in this country. He has published three previous books: *In Memory of My Third Decade*, Footprint Press, 1981; *Turmoil in Hungary: An Anthology of Twentieth-Century Hungarian Poetry in Translation*, New Rivers Press, 1982; and *Memory of Snow: The Selected Poems of Sándor Csoóri*, Penmaen Press, 1983. He is a recipient of the poetry prize for 1984/85 given by the New Jersey Arts Council. He was elected a member of the American Chapter of International P.E.N.

Sándor Csoóri is one of the three finest contemporary poets of Hungary. Eight books of his poetry and eight of his prose have so far seen print. He is a famous essayist; he also writes film scripts. He is well-known not only in Hungary (where he received the prestigious Attila Jozsef Prize for Poetry) but throughout Europe as well. Recently he received Austria's Herder Prize for literature.

Elemér Horváth, a native of Hungary, is a naturalized U.S. citizen. By profession, he is a printer. He has published four books of poetry. He writes exclusively in Hungarian and appears regularly in the foremost European and North American literary magazines that publish in Hungarian.

The photographs in *Reception at the Mongolian Embassy* have been selected from Nicholas Kolumban's personal collection of family portraits and post cards.